Crafty
Inventions

Crafty
Inventions

Crafty
Inventions

Crafty
Inventions

Crafty
Inventions

Crafty
Inventions

suoᴉʇuǝʌuI
ʎʇɟɒɹꓛ

Crafty
Inventions

Crafty
Inventions

suoᴉʇuǝʌuI
ʎʇɟɒɹꓛ

Crafty
Inventions

suoᴉʇuǝʌuI
ʎʇɟɐɹƆ

Crafty
Inventions

Crafty
Inventions

suoᴉʇuǝʌuI
ʎʇɟɐɹƆ

TRADE AND INDUSTRY

by Gerry Bailey

Illustrated by
Jan Smith and
Andrew Keylock

Reading Adviser:
Susan Kesselring, M.A., Literacy Educator
Rosemount-Apple Valley-Eagan
(Minnesota) School District

PICTURE WINDOW BOOKS
www.picturewindowbooks.com

First American edition published in 2005 by
Picture Window Books
5115 Excelsior Boulevard
Suite 232
Minneapolis, MN 55416
877-845-8392
www.picturewindowbooks.com

Publisher: Felicia Law
Design director: Tracy Carrington
Project manager: Karen Foster
Author: Gerry Bailey
Editors: Rosalind Beckman, Christianne Jones, and
Jackie Wolfe
Designed by: Jacqueline Palmer; assisted by Fanny
Level, Will Webster, and Tracy Davies
Cartoon illustrations: Steve Boulter (Advocate)
and Andrew Keylock (Specs Art Agency)

Make-and-do: Jan Smith
Model-maker: Tim Draper
further models: Robert Harvey, Abby Dean
Photo studio: Steve Lumb
Photo research: Diana Morris
Scanning: Acumen Colour
Digital workflow: Edward MacDermott

Library of Congress Cataloging-in-Publication Data
Bailey, Gerry.
Trade and industry / written by Gerry Bailey ;
illustrated by Jan Smith and Andrew Keylock.
p. cm. — (Crafty inventions)
Includes bibliographical references and index.
ISBN 1-4048-1047-1 (hardcover)
1. Technology—Juvenile literature. 2.
Inventions—Juvenile literature. I. Boulter, Steve,
ill. II. Smith, Jan, 1956- ill. III. Keylock, Andrew,
ill. IV. Title. V. Series.

T48.B145 2005
600—dc22   2004024421

Photo Credits
AKG Images: 17t, 25t, 29t, 33t.; Bettmann/
Corbis: 13t, 37t.; Jon Burbank/Hutchison PL:
38b.; Derek Cattani/Eye Ubiquitous: 9t.;
David Cummings/Eye Ubiquitous: 10b.; Mary
Evans PL: 41t.; J. Garrett/Trip: 14b.; David
Keaton/Corbis: 18b.; NASA: 22b.; Nancy
Richmond/The Image Works/Topham: 30b.;
H. Rogers/Trip: 5t.; Science Photo Library:
34b.; Marcus Stace/Eye Ubiquitous: 6b.;
James A. Sugar/Corbis: 21t.; A. Tovy/Trip:
26b.; J Wender/Trip: 42b.

Crafty Inventions

TRADE AND INDUSTRY

Table of Contents

How Can I Take a Picture? 4
How Can I Lift Heavy Weights? 8
How Can I Clean Cotton Quickly? 12
How Can I Explore the Seabed? 16
How Can I See the Stars at Night? 20
How Can I Travel Through the Air? 24
How Can I Save on Journey Time? 28
How Can I See Inside the Body? 32
How Can I Send an Electric Message? 36
How Can I Power a Pulling Vehicle? 40
Glossary 44
Index 47
Tools and Materials 48

How Can I Take a Picture?

William is fascinated by how light makes an image on a wall when it passes through a small hole. But once the light has gone, the image goes as well. William wants to find a way to keep the image. He wants to record the picture the light makes.

William uses a dark room with a small hole in one wall to let light in. The light makes an image on the far wall of what is outside. He wonders how he can get the image to stay permanently on the wall. He thinks a certain kind of wallpaper might work—but it doesn't.

How can I take snapshots?

William makes a smaller box, designed like the room with a hole in one side. The light shines in and hits the far side. But the image it makes disappears as soon as the light stops shining.

WHAT CAN HE DO?

- He could draw around the image made by the light inside his box and color it in. But he'd have to work fast, and what if a cloud blocks the light?

- What if he tried to find a material that is sensitive to light? Perhaps this material would change where the light hits it.

- He could try making a plate of this material for the light to hit. But he'd have to use a new one every time he took a picture—a bit of a waste.

- If he applied a light-sensitive material to paper, it would be flexible and could be moved through the box to make a series of pictures.

I know, I'll use paper coated with silver chloride because it's a chemical that's sensitive to light. The silver will disappear or grow darker where the light hits it. It will leave the same shape as the object reflecting the light.

The first cameras were very large, so they were supported on a tripod. A cloth reduced the amount of light entering the camera.

Taking a photo

A **camera** is a device for taking photographs. Light passes through one or more lenses onto a film coated with silver-based crystals. These make the film sensitive to light. When a picture is taken, the crystals on the film change depending on how much light hits them. This makes a **negative** image, or picture, with dark and light reversed.

The film is then developed to produce a **positive** image that looks just like the original scene. Color film has three layers of light-sensitive chemicals. Each one is sensitive to a different color. The colors combine to form a lifelike color photo. Modern **digital** cameras can take pictures and transfer them immediately to a computer.

Crystals

A **crystal** is a type of solid. All the crystals of a particular substance are the same shape. A crystal of sugar, for example, looks like a tiny cube. A quartz crystal is a **hexagon**, or six-sided shape. Crystals of different substances have different shapes. Crystals are often hard, shiny, and have smooth flat surfaces.

Most **minerals**, the chemicals that are found naturally in the earth or rocks, are made up of hard crystals. An ore is a type of mineral that contains metals such as gold and silver. Some mineral crystals can change, or break down, when exposed to light.

Crystals come in many different colors.

Silver is mixed with other chemicals and used to coat photographic film. When the film is exposed to light in the camera, the crystals in the mixture change to produce an image of the object the camera is photographing.

Inventor's words

camera • crystal
digital • hexagon
mineral • negative
positive

Make a display of negative pictures

You will need

- brush • black cardboard
- white pencil
- white cardboard
- clear acetate
- black, white, and gray paints
- scissors or craft knife
- double-sided tape

1 Draw frames on to black cardboard with a white pencil. Cut out.

2 Cut out acetate panels to fit the frames. Attach with sticky tape.

3 Cut panels of white cardboard to fit. Now draw and paint abstract patterns and swirls in black, gray, and white.

4 Cut out some shapes. If you use a craft knife, ask an adult to help you.

5 Mount the "negative" pictures on the acetate frames.

How Can I Lift Heavy Weights?

Harvey needs to lift heavy pieces of scrap metal. But most of the lifting devices he tries can't take much weight before breaking. Harvey could use a magnet to do the work, but every magnet he tries is just too weak.

Every day, Harvey travels around, collecting pieces of scrap metal. If the piece is small, he has no trouble lifting it into his cart. But if it is large, he has to use a small, crane-like device. This can be awkward, though. More often than not, the piece of metal falls back to the ground, sometimes just missing his foot.

Harvey knows that a magnet will pick up metal. He tries using small bar magnets. He even attaches one to his crane. But the magnets are too weak and cannot lift very heavy loads.

I must find a way to lift all that scrap metal onto my cart.

WHAT CAN HE DO?

- He could hire a few strongmen from the circus. That would be very expensive!

- A magnet would be simpler. But any magnet he uses needs to be very strong. Tying a number of magnets together sounds like a good idea—but it doesn't help.

- He could try using an electric wire with a current running through it. That should produce some magnetism around the wire. But would it be strong enough?

- What about combining the electric wire with the magnets? Together they might produce the power he needs.

This works even better than I thought. Winding electric wire around an iron bar and passing a current through it increases its magnetic force much more than I expected. Now I have a strong electromagnet for my crane.

Electromagnets generate a huge pulling force when an electric current is passed through the wire.

On and off

An **electromagnet** is made up of an iron or steel bar with a coil of wire wrapped around it. The coil is usually made of copper wire because it is an excellent **conductor** of **electricity**. The rod becomes magnetic when an electric **current** is passed through the coil of wire, known as a **solenoid**. Electromagnets work only when a current of electricity moves through the solenoid. When the current is turned off, the rod is no longer magnetized. This means an electromagnet can be turned on and off, unlike a permanent **magnet**. The lines of the magnetic field in an electromagnet loop from the electromagnet's north pole at one end, to its south pole at the other end.

Electricity

Electricity is a type of energy. A current or flow of electricity through an electric circuit, or path, can be used to power televisions, radios, motors, and other devices. The particles that flow along the circuit, which is usually a wire, are called electrons.

An electron is part of a tiny speck of matter called an atom. Each atom has a nucleus, an even smaller particle, at its center, and one or more electrons spinning around it. In some kinds of material, electrons can be made to move away from the nucleus of their atom. They can be pushed from one atom to another. These electrons push other electrons until a flow of electrons is set up. Each electron only has a small amount of energy, but there are millions of electrons inside a single wire, creating a big flow of electricity and a lot of energy.

Electricity is conducted through these overhead wires.

CONDUCTORS

Some materials are better at carrying an electric current than others. These materials are called conductors.

Most metals are good conductors, but materials such as wood and rubber are not. These materials are sometimes used to cover metal wires to keep the electricity in.

Inventor's words

atom • conductor
electric circuit
electric current
electricity
electromagnet
electron • magnet
matter • nucleus
solenoid

Make a battery-powered crane

You will need

- 6V or 9V large battery
- thick cardboard
- heavy paper
- wide postal tube
- craft glue • sticky tape
- copper wire • paper clip
- skewers • large nail
- straw • string
- rubber band

1 Wedge a piece of postal tube over the battery, and cut a hole in a heavy paper lid so the electrical contacts show.

2 Make a stick ladder. Coil wire around each arm of the ladder and wind the bottom ends around the electrical connections. Leave a gap in the wiring on one side for the on/off switch.

3 For the switch, attach a stick to the crane arm with a rubber band. Glue a bit of card and a paper clip to the end of it. When pushed down, the paper clip should connect the wire across the gap.

4 Wrap wire around a nail, then feed one end through a straw and loop to hook over the crane arm. Tape the other wire end to the straw and hook this over the other side of the crane arm. The wires must not touch.

5 Attach a piece of wire to the back of the battery housing and loop. Tie string to the top end of the crane arm, then feed it back through the wire loop and attach the end to a stone weight. Press the "on" switch to pick up metallic loads.

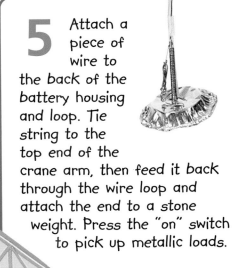

11

How Can I Clean Cotton Quickly?

Eli is studying to be a lawyer. But he is also skilled at making and repairing mechanical devices. He lives in a region where cotton is grown. But getting cotton ready for market is a long and difficult task as the fibers have to be separated from the seeds.

Eli knows that in the cotton fields it takes one person a whole day in the hot sun to "clean," or separate, the seeds from just one fourth a mile of long-staple cotton. But cotton growing is not always profitable. It is also backbreaking work. Short-staple cotton is cheaper and easier to grow, but it's more difficult to clean.

Eli is a guest of Mrs. Green, who admires his mechanical skills. She suggests to some growers that they ask Eli to build a machine to clean short-staple cotton and make their plantations profitable.

How can I separate cotton fibers from the seeds quickly and easily?

WHAT CAN HE DO?

- A giant brush might pull the cotton through. But it would probably be too heavy and awkward to use.

- He could use rollers to squash the cotton seeds out. But that would only work for certain kinds of cotton with loose seeds.

- What if he combined the brush and roller idea? The hairs of the brush would have to be strong. And how would he secure the seeds so they'd come off?

I think I'll cover a cylinder with rows of wire teeth. The teeth will pull the cotton through tiny slots so small, the seeds won't get through. A roller with brushes will remove the cotton fibers from the teeth.

Whitney's gin could clean over 44 pounds (20 kg) of cotton a day—about 50 times the amount a worker could achieve.

Ginning cotton

A **cotton gin** is a machine used to separate and remove cottonseeds from cotton fibers. There are two kinds of cotton gin: a roller gin and a saw gin. In a roller gin, cotton fibers are gripped by rollers and pulled through a space that is too small to let the seeds pass. A saw gin uses a series of circular saws to carry the cotton fibers through a space too narrow for the seeds.

The first simple cotton gins were used in ancient India. A similar kind of gin, the roller gin, was introduced in America in the 1740s—but it could only be used with certain kinds of cotton. Eli Whitney's gin was faster and more economical. By the 1850s, the United States had become the world's largest cotton grower. Much of the cotton was shipped to England to be made into cloth.

13

Rollers

A **roller** is a very wide wheel. It can be used on its own or with one or more rollers to do a job. A single roller made of heavy material is used to make the surface of roads flat and even. Two rollers work together to press water out of clothing. A series of rollers is used in huge **printing presses**.

The first rollers were probably just tree trunks used to transport large objects. They helped reduce **friction**, or rubbing. Later, rollers were used for different jobs such as flattening or pressing materials. Large rollers are used to squeeze iron or steel into thin sheets. Rollers can also be used to move objects. Some conveyor belts are made up of a series of rollers. A **roller bearing** fits between two moving parts of a machine. A roller fits into a space between two rings. It is free to roll as the two parts of the machine, connected to the rings, move.

Rollers press soft steel into sheets.

COTTON

Cotton is a flowering plant that has been grown as a crop for thousands of years. The fluffy seed heads are harvested then spun to make cotton yarn. It is then made into a light material for clothing or other domestic uses.

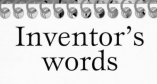

Inventor's words

cotton gin
friction
printing press
roller
roller bearing

Make a woven picture

You will need

- wooden picture frame
- brass tacks
- small hammer
- thin string
- thin strips of colored paper
- pipe cleaners • beads

1 Hammer brass tacks at roughly .4 inch (1 cm) intervals, along two opposite sides of the picture frame. Ask an adult to help you.

2 String up the loom as shown.

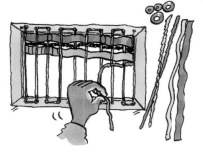

3 Use fine strips of paper, alternated with pipe cleaners, to weave in and out of the string. You can thread on beads as you weave.

4 When your woven picture is finished, hang it up for everyone to admire!

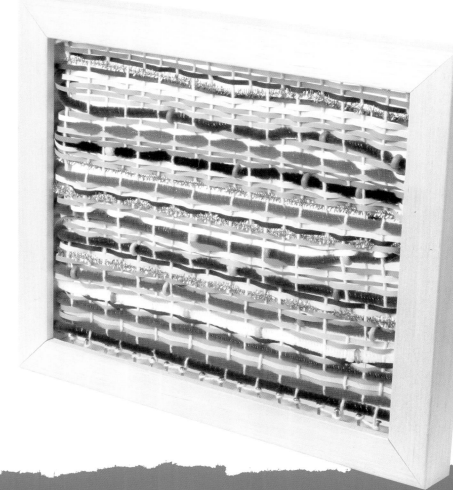

How Can I Explore the Seabed?

Julio knows there is treasure in the old ship that has sunk just offshore. He has read some documents that say it was carrying gold bars. Somehow, he has to get the treasure up. But the ship is about a half mile or so down and Julio needs time under water to explore.

Julio is a good swimmer. He can swim for over a half mile without getting tired. He can't swim very far underwater, though, which makes it impossible for him to spend any time exploring the wreck. Swimming faster doesn't help as he runs out of air quicker.

I need to breathe underwater if I want time to find the treasure.

He tries holding his breath and staying down as long as possible, but the wreck is too far down. He soon needs to come up for air.

WHAT CAN HE DO?

- He could build a waterproof carriage and use seahorses to pull it under the sea. He'd need many, many seahorses.

- A fishbowl upside down over his head might do the trick. It would give him a little air, but probably not enough.

- Perhaps he could find a very long, hollow reed and use that to breathe through. A good idea, but where would he find a reed long enough?

- What about a flexible hose to breathe through? That might be long enough, but it would restrict his movements.

Edmund Halley's diving bell could be lowered 66 feet (20 meters) under the sea. Divers could stay down for about an hour and a half.

Under the sea

A **diving bell** is a large, hollow container that is filled with **air** and is open at the bottom. It is used to carry divers and their tools to work on the ocean floor or the bottom of a river. A pipe at the top of the diving bell allows a supply of air to be pumped into the bell from the surface. The first diving bell to be used was invented by the Italian Guglielmo de Loreno in 1535.

In 1691, Edmund Halley invented a diving bell that was connected by a pipe to weighted barrels of air that could be refilled from the surface. Modern diving bells are usually made of steel and are much more comfortable to work in than the originals. They are equipped with electric lights, communications equipment, and a constant supply of air.

Air

Air is a mixture of gases that make up the atmosphere that surrounds the Earth. Air contains the gases nitrogen, oxygen, argon, and small amounts of carbon dioxide.

Air is a substance that takes up space and has weight. The weight of the air that surrounds the Earth pushes against the surface of everything on the Earth. We call this weight **air pressure**.

Air pressure becomes less the higher into the atmosphere you go. The air pressure on top of a mountain, for instance, is less than the air pressure at the bottom. This is because there is less air pressing on you at the top. Aircraft that travel at 29,700 ft (9,000 m) need special pressurized cabins so that the air pressure inside the plane is the same as that at ground level.

On top of a mountain the air pressure is low. At 52,800 ft (16,000 m), it is only one-tenth of the pressure on the ground.

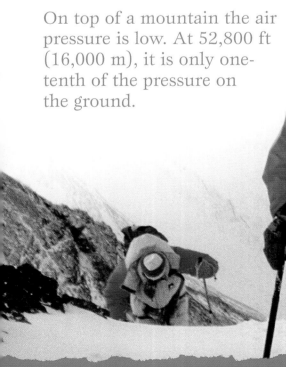

ESSENTIAL GASES

Billions of years ago, when the Earth first formed, there was no atmosphere. Then gases from inside the Earth escaped through volcanoes to form cloudy air. Rain fell, which created oceans, and life began. The first life-forms added oxygen to the atmosphere, which made the air breathable for animals.

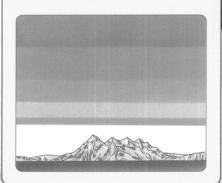

Inventor's words

air
air pressure
atmosphere
diving bell
oxygen

Make a diving bell

You will need

- yogurt containers with lid
- cork, cut in half
- thin plastic tubing
- large plastic squeeze bottle
- square of thin plastic
- stapler
- pebbles, glass beads, or marbles
- oil-based paints • brush
- cut-out cartoon people

1 For the bell, turn the yogurt container upside down. Make a small hole in the top and a larger hole in the bottom.

2 Make a hole through the two corks. Push the ends of the tubing into the corks. Fit tightly.

3 Push one cork end into the top of the bell and the other into the squeeze bottle. Fit tightly.

4 Curl the plastic into a cylinder and staple the flap. Cut and bend out bottom flaps. Staple to the inside of the lid and put back on. Weight the bell with a few pebbles or marbles.

5 Paint the outside of the bell with oil-based paints. Glue on cut-out cartoon people for the divers.

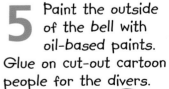

HOW TO USE YOUR DIVING BELL

Squeeze the air out of the bottle and place the diving bell in deep water. It will bob in the water. Allow the bottle to re-inflate, and the bell will sink to the bottom. Squeeze the bottle again to bring the bell to the surface.

How Can I See the Stars at Night?

Isaac wants to find out as much as he can about the stars and planets in the night sky. But the telescopes he has do not give him the view he wants. The images they provide are often unclear, and they are far too small.

In his laboratory, Isaac looks at the sky through a telescope. It is a long tube with lenses at either end. He can see better with the telescope than with the naked eye. But the image he sees is fuzzy around the edges, as if it had a rainbow halo around it.

> I need a telescope that clearly magnifies the stars and planets.

He cannot see the landscape of the Moon clearly enough to tell if there is life there. Nor can he see the planets close enough to discover new moons around them.

WHAT CAN HE DO?

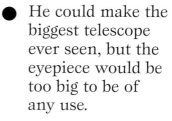

- He could make the biggest telescope ever seen, but the eyepiece would be too big to be of any use.

- What about joining a number of telescopes together to make a very long one? It might get him closer to the objects he's looking at. It would take up a lot of room, though.

- He could use a different kind of lens to concentrate more light in the telescope. That should make a bigger image, but it might not be any clearer.

- How about replacing the lens with something that concentrates light even better—maybe a mirror?

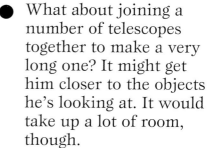

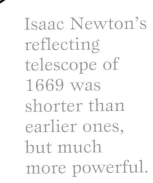

I'll use a mirror in my telescope instead of a series of lenses to magnify the stars. A mirror will reflect and concentrate the light. The light can be reflected to an eyepiece at the side of the telescope, so the images I see will be much clearer.

Isaac Newton's reflecting telescope of 1669 was shorter than earlier ones, but much more powerful.

The night sky

A **telescope** is used for studying objects in the night sky. Reflecting telescopes, those that gather **light**, use mirrors to make a clear image without blurring at the edges. The waves from distant stars are so weak they can only be seen if their light energy is concentrated by a **lens** or mirror. A reflecting telescope uses a mirror to collect and **focus**, or concentrate, light waves.

The place in the telescope where the light is focused is called the **focal point**. Images can also be magnified by the lens at the viewing end of the telescope, called the eyepiece. Today, the largest reflecting telescopes are the Keck telescopes in Hawaii, with mirrors 33 ft (10 m) wide. They are housed in large observatories that open to the sky when the telescopes are in use.

Light waves

Light is a type of energy that is made up of electromagnetic waves. These are the waves we can see with our eyes. Other electromagnetic waves, such as X-rays or ultraviolet rays, cannot be seen.

Until the 20th century, most scientists believed that light only travels in waves, just like ripples that move across a pond. Some, however, like Sir Isaac Newton, believed that light travels in tiny particles he called corpuscles. We now know more about light through the study of modern physics. Today, scientists think that light can be seen to travel either way, depending on how it is measured or observed. So light has the characteristics of both waves and particles.

Most of the light we receive comes from the sun. Never look directly at the sun, as it can damage your eyes.

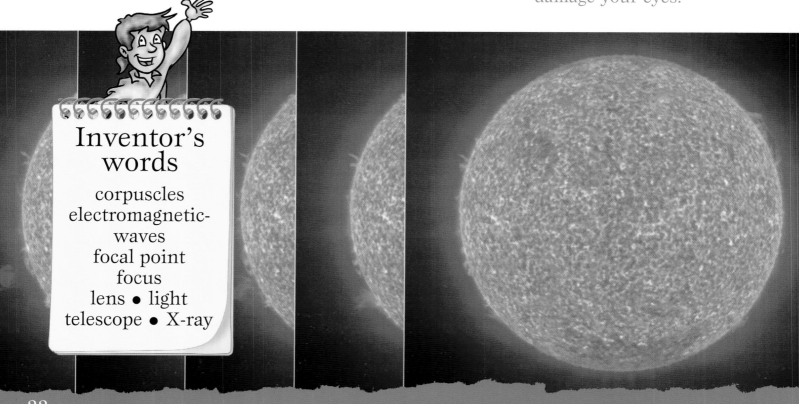

Inventor's words

corpuscles
electromagnetic-
waves
focal point
focus
lens • light
telescope • X-ray

Make your own periscope

You will need
- cardboard • heavy paper
- two small oblong mirrors
- paints • brush
- craft glue
- scissors

1 Score and fold a piece of cardboard to make a large rectangular column. Stick a piece of paper over one end.

2 Cut a flap into the cardboard at the bottom end of the column. Push the flap inward on fold line.

3 Glue a mirror on to the inside of pushed-in panel. Attach at at 45 degree angle.

4 Make another column out of cardboard, slightly larger than the first so that they slide into each other, as shown.

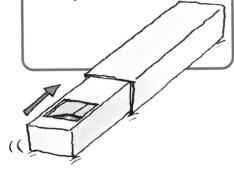

5 Cut a flap into the top end and attach a mirror in the same way. Decorate and slide the two columns together to make a working periscope.

How Can I Travel Through the Air?

Jacques and Joseph work with paper. Among other things, they make paper bags. But their real interest is flying. Both want to see the first human being take to the air like a bird. How to do it, though, is another matter!

The brothers know that people are too heavy to fly on their own. But lighter objects tend to float through the air, even if they eventually come down.

Birds have wings to help them fly. Humans only have arms, so they have to look for a different way.

It's our dream to fly. But how?

In their workshop, the brothers notice that paper bags filled with air float gently to the ground when dropped. But when they are filled with smoke, they rise off the ground.

WHAT CAN THEY DO?

- What if they filled one of their bags with a flock of birds? The birds would make the bag rise—but what a mess!

- If they blew air into the bag, it would move, but it would be impossible to control.

- They could make a large bag, light a fire under it, and see if the smoke makes it rise. Hmm, cold smoke doesn't work!

- Perhaps it's the gases from the fire, not the smoke, that will make the bag rise. How about making a special bag to hold the gases from the fire?

The secret is hot air. Let's make a large cloth bag and line it with paper. We'll light a fire underneath it. As the hot gases enter the bag, they'll rise up. The rising air will push up the bag and we'll have liftoff!

In 1783, the Montgolfier brothers launched their first balloon, carrying a sheep, a rooster, and a duck.

Gas bags

A **hot-air balloon** is a type of aircraft. It is lighter than **air** and cannot be steered. A balloon is made from a large bag called an **envelope**. The first balloons were round, but now balloons are made in almost any shape. The envelope is attached by ropes to a basket, in which the passengers ride.

Most balloons are filled with hot air, generated from a kind of flamethrower under the balloon. Light gases such as helium or **hydrogen** can also be used, although they can be more dangerous. The most important gas balloons are scientific ones, which are used to carry instruments to record the weather.

Molecules

All simple substances are made up of tiny particles called atoms. A molecule is a bigger particle that contains two or more atoms. A molecule of water, for instance, contains two atoms of a gas called hydrogen and one atom of oxygen. Molecules are so small that one drop of tap water contains millions of them.

When molecules are cold, they tend to huddle together. But when they are heated, they speed up and move away from each other. Molecules in hot air, for example, move around faster than molecules in cold air. Faster-moving molecules in hot air take up more space than slower-moving molecules in cold air, so there are fewer of them in the same amount of space. With fewer molecules, the hot air in the space is lighter and so it rises. A hot-air balloon uses speeding molecules to make it rise.

STEAM BALLOON

In 1852, Henri Giffard of France made the first flight in a powered balloon. He used a steam engine and propeller system to push the balloon forward, and a rudder to steer it. It flew at a speed of about 3.1 mph (4.9 km).

Modern balloons use hot air warmed by a propane fire to make them rise.

Inventor's words

air • atom
envelope
hot-air balloon
hydrogen
molecule
oxygen

Make a balloon mobile

You will need
- balloon • string
- newspaper • craft glue
- paint • colored paper
- small box
- fabric
  or carpet scraps
- sticky tape
- pins or thumbtacks
- plastic spoons

1 Hang a balloon from a string. Cover it with layers of pieces of newspaper soaked in craft glue mixed with water. Dry between layers.

2 Paint and decorate the balloon.

3 Cover a small box in fabric or carpet.

4 Cut eight pieces of string and tie a knot at one end of each. Attach the knotted ends to the inside of the balloon basket with sticky tape.

5 Stick eight pins or thumbtacks around the base of the balloon. Wind the other end of the pieces of string around the pins or thumbtacks and glue. Make passengers by painting faces onto plastic spoons.

How Can I Save on Journey Time?

It's a long way from Hector's house to town. He has to go to town twice a day to visit his ailing aunt. He could manage one journey on foot. But often he has to wait for a ride to make the second trip. Sometimes he doesn't get a ride, but he can't stop making the journeys.

Hector could walk more slowly and save energy. It might make it easier for him to do the second journey, but this would make him late.

He cannot ride the family horse as it's too old and couldn't carry him as far as the village—even once.

He could always wait for a lift before making the journey. But if no one comes by, he will never get to his destination. And he cannot afford to buy a cart or a new horse.

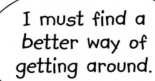

I must find a better way of getting around.

WHAT CAN HE DO?

- He could saddle up his prize pig and ride it to the village. But that would be an even slower journey.

- If he made a sail out of a piece of cloth and attached it to the pig, it might go faster. But it would be too difficult to control.

- Perhaps he could try and rebuild the old cart in the stable. Two wheels on one side are in good shape, but the ones on the other side are broken.

- If he attached the two wheels to a frame, he might be able to make some sort of vehicle on which to ride, but it would have no power.

I'll use my own power. I'll attach two wheels, one in front of the other, on a thin frame. I'll make the front wheel pivot on the frame and put a handle on it to steer with. I'll throw a saddle over the middle part. Then I can hop on and push with my feet.

A hobbyhorse was propelled by pushing the feet on the ground. It became very fashionable during the early 19th century.

Bike ride

A **bicycle** is a vehicle that has a frame and two wheels, one behind the other. The wheels move when the rider pushes against pedals, which are attached by a chain to the rear wheel. The bicycle is steered by handles that join the front part of the frame and turn the front wheel. The first bicycle was called a **hobbyhorse**.

It was invented around 1800. It had to be pushed along by the rider's feet. The first pedal bicycle was called a **velocipede**. It was made of wood with iron-covered wheels. It was known as a "boneshaker" because it had no springs and roads were bumpy. Modern bikes have springs and **gears** to make riding easier and more comfortable.

Gears

A gear is a wheel or disk with grooves cut into the edge. Gears work in pairs. The teeth of one gear mesh, or fit snugly, into the teeth of the other. When one gear turns, it moves the second gear in the opposite direction. A gear is a way of sending power from one part of a machine to another.

If both gears are the same size, the wheels turn at the same speed. If one is bigger than the other, the gear wheels can be used to speed up or slow down movement. They can also be used to increase or decrease force.

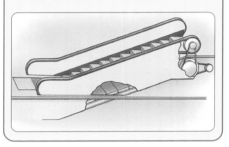

BELT DRIVE

A belt can be used in the same way as gears. When a belt is attached between two wheels, it transfers power from one to the other. A fan belt in a car, for example, transfers power from the engine to the fan. Speed can be changed by altering the size of one of the wheels.

When a large wheel is attached to a smaller one, the larger wheel will make the smaller wheel turn faster. A bicycle has a number of different-sized gears attached to the rear wheel. The smaller the gear, the faster the bike will go when it is pedaled, but the more effort it takes to turn the pedals.

A gear system helps to make the best use of a car's power.

Inventor's words

bicycle
gear
hobbyhorse
mesh
velocipede

Make a spinning bike path

You will need

- toilet paper tubes
- shallow box
- thick and thin cardboard
- wooden dowels
- coat hanger • cardboard
- pipe cleaners • glue
- rubber band • scissors

1 Glue toilet paper tubes to the *base* of a box to make a table. Cut a hole at each end.

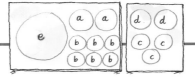

2 Cut one large circle, two medium circles, and six small circles from thick cardboard. Now cut two medium and three small circles from thin cardboard.

3 Make a hole in the middle of each circle and thread them onto two dowels like this. Push the dowels through the holes in the tabletop.

4 Push coat hanger wire through the smaller circle stack, attach firmly, and bend into a handle shape. Make a cardboard pedal.

5 Make bicycles out of pipe cleaners and glue them onto the larger circle stack.

6 Put a large rubber band around both circle stacks to make a drive belt. Now turn the pedal to spin the bikes.

You can change gear by moving the rubber band from the large circle to the small circle on the pedal side.

How Can I See Inside the Body?

Wilhelm is a scientist. He has set up an experiment to study gas. The experiment has given him some useful information. However, he has noticed that something unexpected is happening in his experiment. It could be dangerous, but his curiosity is aroused.

Wilhelm has set up his experiment to see what happens when an electric current is passed through a tube of gas. Perhaps the gas will light up or become hot. Perhaps something else will happen.

Then he notices that some chemicals on the other side of the room are glowing in the dark. When he switches off the electricity, they stop glowing. Some kind of ray must be coming out of the tube.

I wonder what this ray is and where it's coming from.

WHAT CAN HE DO?

- He could use a giant portable microscope to try and see the rays as they came out of the tube.

- Perhaps he could try and catch the rays in a container. But what would he make the container out of, and how will he know when the rays are in it?

- If he studies the rays, he might find out what else they can do besides lighting up the chemicals.

- He might find that they pass through soft objects like cardboard, but are absorbed by hard ones like bone. But what could he use them for?

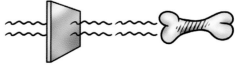

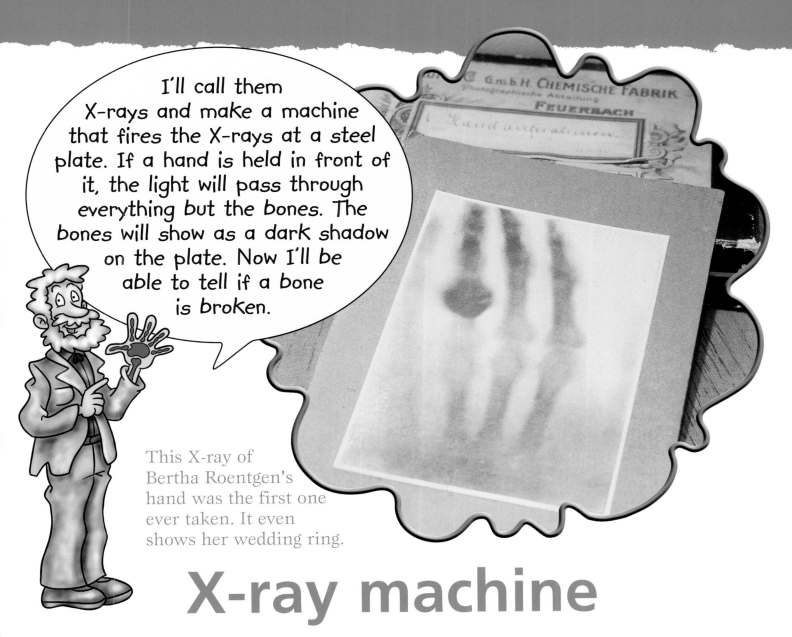

I'll call them X-rays and make a machine that fires the X-rays at a steel plate. If a hand is held in front of it, the light will pass through everything but the bones. The bones will show as a dark shadow on the plate. Now I'll be able to tell if a bone is broken.

This X-ray of Bertha Roentgen's hand was the first one ever taken. It even shows her wedding ring.

X-ray machine

An **X-ray** machine, or radiography machine, uses X-rays, invisible rays of energy, to take pictures of heavy material such as bones inside the body. X-ray machines are also used in industry to look inside substances to see if they are broken or have flaws. Wilhelm Roentgen, a German scientist, discovered X-rays quite by chance in 1895. He named the new rays "X" to indicate they were unknown.

Radiation, the X-ray waves that pass through the air, is directed from the X-ray machine. The waves pass through the patient and hit a piece of photographic film. Because X-rays are absorbed by heavy objects, the rays that hit bone don't pass through to the film. This leaves a dark patch on it. All the other rays pass through and make the rest of the film light. So the film shows a picture of just the bone.

Electromagnetism

Electromagnetic radiation, or waves, is a form of energy that travels at the speed of light. Radio waves, microwaves, light, and X-rays are all kinds of electromagnetic radiation. Each one creates both an electric and magnetic field as it moves.

The energy of an electromagnetic wave changes with its wavelength. A wavelength is the distance from the top of one wave to the top of the next wave. The shorter the wavelength, the more energy it has. Gamma rays have the shortest wavelength, and so the most energy. Radio waves have the longest wavelength and the least energy. X-rays have the next shortest wavelength to gamma rays, so they have a great deal of energy. They can be dangerous to people if not used with care.

The electromagnetic spectrum is a chart that lists the different kinds of radiation in order of their wavelengths.

CATS

A Computerized Axial Tomographic scanner, known as a CAT scanner, is another device that lets doctors see inside the body.

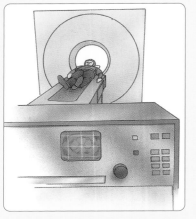

It traces heat sources in the brain and shows them as an image doctors can study.

Ne397 Ca395 H410 H434 H486 H486 O501 Mg517 Na589 O630 H656 H656 S672

400   500   600   700   800   900   100

Inventor's speak

electric field
electromagnetic-
radiation
magnetic field
radiation
wavelength
X-ray

Make skeleton leaf prints

You will need

- selection of leaves
- black and colored cardboard
- glue • paint
- double-sided sticky tape

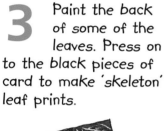

1 Arrange leaves of different shapes and sizes to make leaf people. Glue them on to thick cardboard.

2 Cut out oblong pieces of black cardboard to cover the middle section of each leaf character.

3 Paint the back of some of the leaves. Press on to the black pieces of card to make 'skeleton' leaf prints.

4 Curve the leaf prints and stick over the characters' 'tummies' with double-sided sticky tape. Paint a face on the heads of your leaf people.

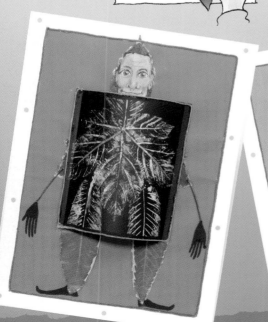

How Can I Send an Electric Message?

Samuel is an artist and doesn't earn much from his paintings. He wants to find a way to make enough to live on while he paints. Perhaps he can use his interest in electricity and communications to invent something useful.

Samuel knows that, somehow, electricity can be used to transmit information. He is aware that it is possible to store electricity in a battery. But stored electricity doesn't go anywhere. He needs to transmit electricity from one place to another.

How can I use electricity to send messages?

He studied science at the university, so he sets up a laboratory to experiment with his ideas. Others have used semaphore systems to send messages. Could these be used with electricity?

WHAT CAN HE DO?

- He could find a way to store a message in a battery, then send the battery by horse to where he wants the message to go. Well, he might as well write a letter.

- He could experiment with bits of wire. Electricity flows through wire. But how would it know what to say?

- What about sending the electricity through the wire in bursts? But they still wouldn't mean anything—unless he used some kind of code.

- Perhaps he could set up a series of telegraph towers and hang wires between them. He can't afford it, though, and he still can't make electricity "talk".

I'll make a code using dots and dashes for each letter. A short or long burst of electricity can represent dots and dashes. I'll persuade the government to give me money to build a wire system using poles, not towers.

The U.S. government gave Morse $30,000 to build the first telegraph line between New York and Washington.

Dots and dashes

A **telegraph** is a device for sending messages over a long distance. The messages are sent along a wire in a code that is made up of bursts of electricity. The operator taps out these bursts with a **transmitter**—a key or fingerpad. Messages are received on paper tape as a series of marks. Samuel Morse developed a code called **Morse Code** to translate the bursts of electricity.

A short burst stood for a dot. A burst three times longer stood for a dash. The message in Morse Code is received on the tape as a series of dots and dashes. The letters most used have the easiest signs. There are also signs for punctuation marks as well as words such as "error." The letters SOS—three dots, three dashes, three dots—form the international distress signal.

Circuits

An electric current is a flow of electricity. It is made up of electrons, the tiny negative charged particles that move around an atom's nucleus, which flow through a conductor. A conductor is a substance that lets electricity flow easily through it. A battery or electricity generator makes the electric current flow.

An electric current flows along a path called an electric circuit. Circuits are usually made of copper wires or cables, as copper is a good conductor. Circuits link electrical components together. In a telegraph system, the flow of electrons, or electric current, travels along wires that are carried on wooden poles or are sunk underground. The tap of a telegraph transmitter sends the electron flow along the wire in short or long bursts.

CIRCUIT BOARD

Modern electronic equipment such as a television or computer often uses a circuit board.

This is a plate made of fiberglass covered with thin copper strips. The strips work in the same way as wires to carry the flow of electrons.

Telegraph poles stretch across a plain carrying messages to remote places.

Inventor's words

atom
conductor
electric current
electric circuit
electron
Morse Code
telegraph
transmitter

Make a Morse code game

1 Cut a large circle of cardboard or foam board. Cover one side with foil and the other with black paper.

2 On the foil side of the circle, draw the Morse code with a black marker.

3 Cut the neck off the plastic bottle and snip a slot in the top of it to hold the Morse code circle. Decorate the handle and slot the circle in.

HOW TO USE:

Play with a partner.
Off position: turn bottle so the code is facing you in order to interpret sent messages.
On position: turn bottle to transmit message, using the code as reference.

OFF   ON

THE MORSE CODE

A • —	M — —	Y — • — —
B — • • •	N — •	Z — — • •
C — • — •	O — — —	0 — — — — —
D — • •	P • — — •	1 • — — — —
E •	Q — — • —	2 • • — — —
F • • — •	R • — •	3 • • • — —
G — — •	S • • •	4 • • • • —
H • • • •	T —	5 • • • • •
I • •	U • • —	6 — • • • •
J • — — —	V • • • —	7 — — • • •
K — • —	W • — —	8 — — — • •
L • — • •	X — • • —	9 — — — — •

How Can I Power a Pulling Vehicle?

Richard is a British engineer. He lives at a time when factories are manufacturing more and more goods. These goods have to be transported to where they are needed. The roads are no longer good enough, so Richard wants to find a better way.

The coal mines and cloth manufacturers, as well as many other businesses, need to get their produce to ports and cities around the country. But the roads are so rough and badly surfaced that the wagon journeys are slow, and no one can tell how long it will take.

Wagons have to be pulled by horses or oxen, one at a time. Even barges on the canals need help. More goods could be transported if a train of wagons could make a journey. If only that were possible!

How can I make a form of transportation that's fast, regular, and reliable?

WHAT CAN HE DO?

- He could harness 50 horses to a wagon train. It would carry more goods, but all those hooves would damage the roads even more.

- Perhaps he could breed super-muscular horses to pull two or three wagons each. But it would take too long and he needs something now.

- What if he harnessed an engine of some sort to a wagon—something with the strength of five horses?

- A steam engine could be attached to a wagon. But it still doesn't solve the problem of the miserable road system.

What if my steam-engine locomotive were to run on rails? That's it! A whole train of wagons can *be* pulled smoothly along a specially-made steel railroad. Steam power will pull carriages full of people and manufactured goods.

Trevithick's public demonstration of his locomotive in London

Steam power

Steam engines were developed during the 18th century. A steam **locomotive** is a vehicle that is powered by a steam engine. The pressure of the steam pushes against a **piston** inside a **cylinder** at the side of the locomotive. The cylinder slides backward and forward inside the piston. The piston is attached by a rod, or crankshaft, and an oval-shaped plate, called a **cam**, to large driving wheels.

As the crankshaft moves backward and forward, it pushes around the cam, which turns the wheels. Richard Trevithick built the first steam locomotive in 1804, which he called Catch Me Who Can. It was improved upon by George Stephenson, who built the famous "Rocket" locomotive, which won the Rainhill speed trials in 1829. He helped to build many of the first railways to be used by the public.

Steam engine

A steam engine is a machine that uses heat energy. It contains a boiler in which water is heated until it reaches boiling point and produces steam. The steam creates pressure that is used to move a piston in a cylinder. The steam pushes the piston down. The movement of the piston can be used to move a lever up and down or turn a wheel.

The Scotsman James Watt designed the first really efficient steam engine in the 1760s. The first steam engines were used to pump water out of mines. Steam engines were also used to power steam hammers, where a heavy piece of metal is driven down on to a flat anvil by the piston. It is used to forge iron and steel. This invention, as well as the steam locomotive and other machines, show how important the development of the steam engine was to the **Industrial Revolution**.

AEOLIPILE

An aeolipile was a very early kind of steam turbine. It was invented as a toy by the Greek scientist Hero of Alexandria. Jets of steam are used to make a ball-shaped boiler rotate, or turn around. The steam comes out of tubes at the side of the boiler, spinning it around.

This turbine uses steam to turn huge blades. The spinning blades create electricity.

Inventor's words

cam
cylinder
Industrial Revolution
locomotive
piston
steam engine

Make a piston-driven boat

You will need

- cardboard
- cardboard tubes
- dowels • tubing
- copper wire
- rubber bands
- cut-out boat
- glue • scissors

1 Make a cardboard wall and base. Glue together.

2 Cut a thick circle from the cardboard and glue to one end of a narrow cardboard tube. Glue a dowel to the edge of the circle. Cut a hole into the wall at one side and push the tubing through. Now push a piece of dowel through the other end of the tube to make a cranking handle.

3 Push a dowel through the other end of the wall, at the same height as the tubing. Hang a small tube from it with wire. Thread a long dowel through this, attaching one end to the dowel on the circle.

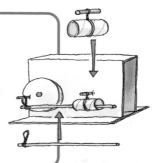

4 Attach a smaller dowel to the first with wire. Push two small dowels through the wall at the top. Lock the smaller dowel into an upright position with a rubber band.

5 Glue a cut-out steam boat to the top of the dowel and decorate your model to look like an ocean bottom.

HOW TO USE:

Turn the handle behind the wall and watch the boat toss on the waves!

Glossary

Air Mixture of gases that makes up our atmosphere. Air contains nitrogen, argon, and small amounts of carbon dioxide.

Air pressure Pressure caused by the weight of the air that surrounds the Earth. It is a force that pushes against the surfaces of all things on the Earth.

Atmosphere Layer of gases that surround the Earth, containing air mixed with water vapor.

Atom Tiny part of an element, or simple substance, made up of an electron or electrons that move around a nucleus. The nucleus is made up of neutrons and protons. All the atoms in an element are the same.

Bicycle Vehicle with a metal frame and two wheels, one behind the other. A rider, who pushes two pedals around, powers the wheels.

Cam Type of wheel that is not circular. One half of its circumference is egg-shaped. Cams are used in machines to move rods up and down.

Camera Device for creating images, or pictures, on paper. It uses a lens to focus light on light-sensitive film. The film is developed to make the image.

Conductor Material that allows heat or electricity to flow easily through it.

Corpuscles A cell or other small rounded body.

Cotton gin Machine designed to remove cotton fibers from cotton seeds. A gin may use rollers or a saw to separate the fibers from the seed.

Crystal Solid with a regular shape such as a cube or hexagon. All crystals of one type have the same shape. Different types of crystal have different shapes.

Cylinder A solid shape that has two ends that are flat and circular. In a machine, it is a hollow tube that has a piston moving up and down inside it.

Digital Device that uses numbers. Data flows through a computer as a series of numbers.

Diving bell Equipment that allows people to work or explore under water. It is shaped like a bell with an open bottom. Air is pumped in from the surface through a hose.

Electric circuit Path along which an electric current flows. It is usually a copper wire or cable.

Electric current Flow of electricity made up of electrons moving through a conductor.

Electric field Area influenced by electromagnetic waves as they move.

Electricity Type of energy used as an electric current to power things.

Electromagnet Coil of wire wrapped around an iron or steel bar. The bar becomes magnetic when an electric current is passed through the wire.

Electromagnetic radiation Type of energy made up of electrical energy and magnetic energy that moves in the form or rays, or waves.

Electromagnetic waves Waves of radiation including light, radio, X-rays, and gamma rays that make up the electromagnetic spectrum.

Electron Tiny speck of matter that is usually part of an atom. An electron moves in a kind of orbit around the nucleus of an atom.

Envelope Part of a balloon. It is a hollow bag that can be filled with light gas such as helium or hot air.

Focal point Point at which parallel rays of light are brought together by a lens that curves inwards.

Focus Make an image or picture clear by controlling the position of lenses in a camera.

Friction Rubbing of two moving objects against each other, which causes them to slow down and generate heat.

Gear Type of wheel with cogs, or projections, around its rim. The cogs of one gear fit into those of another, so one gear can drive another.

Hexagon Flat shape with six sides.

Hobby horse Early bicycle without pedals.

Hot air balloon Type of aircraft that is lighter than air and cannot be steered. It is made up of a large bag, or envelope, filled with light gas and attached by ropes to a basket.

Hydrogen Colorless gas. It is the lightest of all the elements and occurs on Earth mainly in combination with oxygen as water.

Industrial Revolution Period of time during the last half of the 18th century and first half of the 19th, during which huge advances were made in science, engineering, and transport. This caused a great change in society from being mostly agricultural to mostly industrial.

Lens Piece of glass or plastic that has been ground so that both sides curve either inwards or outwards. It is used to bend light.

Light Type of energy. Light is made up of electromagnetic waves that can be seen by the human eye. Light waves are found at the middle of the electromagnetic spectrum.

Locomotive Powerful vehicle that moves a train on rails. It can be powered by steam, electricity or diesel.

Magnet Object, usually of metal, that attracts other metal objects. It has a positive and negative pole.

Magnetic field Area affected by the magnetic force between the north and south poles of a magnet.

Matter Everything in the universe that occupies space and has weight. Matter can be a solid, liquid, or gas.

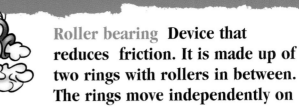

Mesh To fit the cogs of one gear snugly into the cogs of another.

Mineral Type of solid such as ore or rock. It is an inorganic, or non-living, material found in the Earth's crust and is usually made up of crystals.

Molecule Small particle containing two or more atoms that are joined together. A molecule of water has two atoms of hydrogen and one atom of oxygen.

Morse code Code invented by Samuel Morse consisting of dots and dashes. It is made up of pulses of electricity and used with the telegraph system.

Negative Picture with the dark and light areas reversed.

Nucleus Center of an atom containing protons and neutrons.

Oxygen Chemical element. It is a colorless gas that is found in the atmosphere.

Piston Tube-like device that fits snugly into a cylinder and moves backwards and forwards. Pistons are used in internal combustion engines and pumps.

Positive Picture that has been printed from a negative to produce an image that is an exact copy of the original scene.

Radiation Type of energy. It is the movement of electromagnetic waves and photons.

Roller Round, cylindrical part of a roller bearing.

Roller bearing Device that reduces friction. It is made up of two rings with rollers in between. The rings move independently on the rollers. It can be fitted to a wheel and axle.

Solenoid Coil of wire wrapped around a magnetic bar. When electricity is passed through the wire, the bar becomes magnetized and moves.

Steam engine Engine powered by steam. The force of moving steam pushes a piston in a cylinder. The backwards and forwards movement of the piston turns a wheel.

Telegraph Machine that sends messages over long distances. Morse code is used to translate words into electrical pulses, which are sent along a wire.

Telescope Instrument that makes distant objects seem closer. It uses lenses or mirrors to magnify objects such as stars or planets.

Transmitter Device used to send radio waves. The waves carry radio or television signals to a receiver.

Velocipede Early bicycle with pedals.

Wavelength Distance between the peak of one electromagnetic wave and the peak of the next.

X-ray Type of electromagnetic wave with a short wavelength. X-rays have great energy and can travel through some materials, such as skin and flesh. They can be used to help treat disease. Also the photographs made by an X-ray machine.

Index

aeolipiles, 42
air, 16, 17, 18, 25, 26
air pressure, 18
atoms, 10, 26, 38

balloons, 24, 25, 26
belt drives, 30
bicycles, 29-30

cameras, 5, 6
CAT (Computerized Axial Tomographic) scanners, 34
circuit boards, 38
circuits, 38
codes, 37
conductors, 9, 10, 38
cotton, 12-13, 14
cotton gins, 13
crystals, 6

Daguerre, Louis, 6
daguerreotype, 6
diving bells, 17

electricity, 9, 10, 36, 38
electromagnetic waves, 22, 34
electromagnetism, 9, 34
electromagnets, 9
electrons, 10, 38

flying, 24-25, 26

gamma rays, 34
gases, 18, 24, 25, 26
gears, 29-30
Giffard, Henri, 26

Greeks, ancient, 42

Halley, Edmund, 17
Hero of Alexandria, 42
hobby horses, 29
hot air balloons, 24, 25

India, 13
Industrial Revolution, 42

light, 4, 5, 21, 22
light waves, 22
locomotives, 41
Loreno, Guglielmo de, 17

magnetism, 8-9, 34
magnets, 8-9
messages, 37
minerals, 6
molecules, 26
Montgolfier brothers, 25
Morse, Samuel, 36-37

Newton, Sir Isaac, 20, 21, 23

oxygen, 18

photography, 4-5, 6

radiation, 33
radio rays, 34
reflecting telescopes, 21
Roentgen, Wilhelm, 32-33
roller bearings, 14
rollers, 13, 14

silver, 5, 6

speed of light, 22
stars, 20-21
steam balloons, 26
steam engines, 40-42
Stephenson, George, 41

telegraph, 37, 38
telescopes, 20-21
toys, 42
transportation, 24, 25, 26, 29-30, 40-42
Trevithick, Richard, 40, 41

underwater exploration, 16-17

velocipedes, 29

Watt, James, 42
wavelengths, 34
weights, lifting, 8-9
Whitney, Eli, 13

x-rays, 32-33, 34

Tools and Materials

Almost all of the materials in this book can be found around the house or bought at your local art or craft shop. If you cannot find the exact item, try to replace it with something similar.

Most of the models will stick fast with craft glue or even wallpaper paste. However, some materials need a stronger glue, so be careful when using these as they may damage your clothes and even your skin. Ask an adult to help you.

Always protect furniture with newspaper or a large cloth, and cover your clothes by wearing an apron.

User Care

Take special care when handling sharp tools such as scissors, pointed gadgets, pieces of wire, or craft knives. Ask an adult to help you when you need to use them.